THOU ART EXALTED
ministries, inc.

"HE CALLS HIS OWN SHEEP BY NAME AND LEADS THEM OUT." JOHN 10:3

He knows my name

Ages 10-14

20/20 mini Lessons
FOR GIRLS!
-with FIVE art Projects-

annie pajcic

THOUARTEXALTED, INC.

Creating Art through God's Word Ministries, INC.
www.thouartexalted.com

He Knows My Name: 20/20 Mini Lessons for Girls
Text copyright © 2015 by Annie Pajcic

ISBN: 978-0989614139

Art Direction, Interior Composition, and Design by:
Annie Pajcic © 2015.

Welcome to: HE KNOWS MY NAME
—20/20 Mini Lessons for Girls!

"The Lord is my shepherd, I lack nothing.
He makes me lie down in green pastures,
he leads me beside quiet waters,
he refreshes my soul.
He guides me along the right paths
for his name's sake." Psalm 23:1-3 (NLT)

Would you describe your life as quiet or busy?

Psalm 23 tells us that the Good Shepherd will lead us beside quiet waters. Notice it does not say "busy" or "rushing" waters! Heaven knows we are all busy and often do not take the time to be still and learn from God. *He Knows My Name: 20/20 Mini Lessons for Girls* will intentionally slow us down and lead us to those quiet places where we can get to know the Good Shepherd.

God knows everything about us. He knows our personalities, our talents, our thoughts, and even how many hairs we have on our heads! But how well do we know Him? Did you know that God calls us His sheep in Scripture? The imagery of sheep and shepherds is used more than 250 times in the Bible. Through this devotional study, we will learn why. I promise you will love it!

He Knows My Name: 20/20 Mini Lessons for Girls will take you to Sheep's Corner to study Scripture. You will ask questions at Sheep's Talk, seek advice from Shepherd's Staff, and learn fun characteristics about sheep at Flock Facts. You can also choose to go deeper with More to Chew. I am so excited you will be joining me to learn more about why we are called sheep in the Bible and why we need the Good Shepherd to lead us everyday. Sheep are not the brightest animals on earth—neither are we sometimes. We, too, need the Good Shepherd to protect us from danger, lead us to safe pasture, feed us, and be our strength when we are weak.

Did I mention the art projects? After four lessons there will be an art opportunity. That's why we are called Thou**ART**exalted—creating art through God's Word. I can't wait for you to creatively learn more about the Good Shepherd.

I am praying for you, so please keep in touch (and send me pictures of your projects!). You can contact me at annie@thouartexalted.com.

With joy,

Annie

Annie Pajcic
Founder and President of ThouArtExalted Ministries, Inc.

How to have a Quiet Time using

HE KNOWS MY NAME
—20/20 Mini Lessons for Girls!

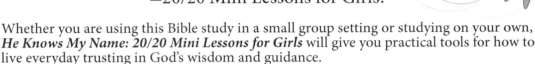

Whether you are using this Bible study in a small group setting or studying on your own, *He Knows My Name: 20/20 Mini Lessons for Girls* will give you practical tools for how to live everyday trusting in God's wisdom and guidance.

The first step in getting to know the Good Shepherd is finding a quiet space to read your Bible and answer the questions. This is not always an easy task, at least not in our household! God can't wait to spend time with you, but you have to make the effort to be still and listen. This is called having a "Quiet Time." It is time spent with God, one-on-one, without distraction to learn more about being a sheep in His fold.

Read this verse from The Message:

> "Find a quiet, secluded place so you won't be tempted to role-play before God. Just be there as simply and honestly as you can manage. The focus will shift from you to God, and you will begin to sense his grace" Matthew 6:6 (MSG).

God wants to have a personal relationship with you, but it's your choice to spend time with Him. Just like a friend you want to get to know, God wants to spend time with you. Turn off your phone and don't check your messages. Grab a pen, your Bible, and start reading the verse that begins each lesson. ThouArtExalted wants you to be filled with these promises:

God made you for a purpose.
  He has a plan for you that is good.
  He will never leave you by yourself.
  He will never forget you.
  He is always watching out for your best interest.

The Good Shepherd cares for you.
  You are not an accident. You are not a mistake.
  You have been given special talents only YOU have.
  You have a special mission on this earth.
  You are here for a reason.

Jesus loves you.
  He calls you His friend.
  He calls you His daughter.
  He calls you His beloved.
  He calls you His masterpiece.
  HE CALLS YOU BY NAME.

  We love you, too! And we have been praying for you — by NAME. Now it's God's turn to shower His love on you. Have fun, open your hearts, and listen. God has something to tell you today!

  ~The ThouArtExalted Team!

TABLE OF CONTENTS

HE KNOWS MY NAME

"He calls his own sheep by name and leads them out."

John 10:3

SHEEP'S CORNER

The word for "calls" in John 10:3 is an actual term for the naming of sheep. Shepherds take this duty very seriously. Why? Because they love their sheep and by giving them an individual name, they are giving them **individual significance.** Names are very important. Think about your name. Why were you named Sarah, or Margaret, or Wentworth Grace? Chances are, you were named after one of your great, great, great grandmothers! Sheep were often named after the environment in which they were born. For example, if a little lamb was born on a beautiful day, the shepherd might name her Joy! Perhaps Joy's sister was named flopsy because her ears were floppy. Maybe one sheep was named socks because she had black legs with a white body. Whatever the case may be, having a name is very important.

> Gretchen felt lost at her new school. She had just moved from a different state and was missing all of her friends. Gretchen did not know anyone except one girl who was the daughter of her mom's roommate in college. But really? How was she going to find Beth Anne in a class of 350 students? She had only met her once before. Gretchen doubted Beth Anne would even recognize her, much less remember her name. Then, out of a sea of people, she heard her name. "Gretchen! Gretchen!" Beth Anne called. "Come on over here and meet some of my friends. We have saved you a seat at our table!" Gretchen lifted her head and smiled. She felt her confidence rise and with excitement, quickly made her way over to Beth Anne's table.

How great is it when someone remembers your name? The Bible tells us that God never forgets our name. In fact, Isaiah 49:16 says, "See, I have written your name on the palms of my hands." How cool is that? The Good Shepherd KNOWS our name, and He never forgets it. The Good Shepherd knows that we, too, have significance. He created us as His masterpiece (Ephesians 2:10). He knows how many hairs we have on our head (Matthew 10:30). He knows the thoughts we think, when we sit and when we rise, and the days ahead (Psalm 139). You are special and significant. Yes, the Good Shepherd knows your name.

1. How did you get your name? Is there a special story behind your birth? If you were a sheep, what would be your name?

----

2. Can you remember a time when someone remembered your name? How did this make you feel?

----

3. Why do you think it's important to remember that God knows your name? What is significant about God leading us?

MORE TO CHEW: God Calls us by Name ~ Isaiah 43:1, John 10:14-15, Psalm 91:14

SHEPHERD'S STAFF

FLOCK FACTS

A GOOD SHEPHERD KNOWS THE NAMES OF HIS FLOCK. THEY ARE NAMED BY THE PERSONAL CHARACTERISTICS OF EACH SHEEP. THE SHEEP HEAR THEIR NAME AND THEY LISTEN TO THE SHEPHERD'S VOICE TO LEAD THEM. THEY WILL NOT FOLLOW A STRANGER'S VOICE.

Not only does God know your name, but He also calls you by name and leads you to safe pastures. We are not a number in a crowd or a face in a room. **We have significance.** But in order for God to lead us, we have to learn how to listen for His voice. How? We hear God's voice by reading the Bible. The more we get to **know** Him, the better we will be at discerning His voice. By knowing God's commands in Scripture and building a relationship with Him, we will know what is right and what is wrong. His voice is not going to be audible, but we will sense the right direction in our hearts. This is called the leading of the Holy Spirit that we receive when we believe in Jesus. Remember, God will never lead us into danger, poor decisions, or sinful actions. He will only lead us into green pasture and quiet waters. Build a genuine relationship with the Good Shepherd. Listen for your name. He loves you personally and leads you out.

Dear Lord, thank You that You know my name! Even before I was born, You knew the days of my life. Because You know the road ahead, I trust You to lead me in the direction You want for me. This can be hard, Lord. I like to go my own way and lead my own life. I guess I feel like I am more in control. I commit to knowing You better by studying Your Word and doing what it says. I trust in Your lead. Guide my steps today and thank You for not calling me flopsy! I love You. Amen.

WE ARE HIS SHEEP

"Know that the LORD is God. It is he who made us, and we are his; we are his people, the sheep of his pasture."

Psalm 100:3

". . . Be still, and know that I am God . . . ."

Psalm 46:10

SHEEP'S CORNER

Psalm 100:3 tells us to "Know that the Lord is God. God made us, and we are his, we are his people, the sheep of his pasture." But how do we get to know God? That seems like a really BIG task! Think about how you might get to know someone. The first step is **meeting** them, right? Has anyone ever said to you, "Have you ever met Michelle?" You might respond, "No, I haven't. But I have heard so much about her, and I really want to meet her!" Do you see the connection? In order to know God, we have to **meet** Him personally and meet with Him continually.

Katie heard about Michelle the day she moved to town. I mean, who hadn't' heard about the new girl on the block? Michelle was the oldest of five kids and her Dad was the coach of the high school football team. Michelle seemed kind, smart, and of course, athletic. But there was something more about her that Katie wanted to know. Michelle's mother died from cancer when she was only 11, and now she was helping raise her four younger siblings. She seemed to be strong and somehow more mature than most of Katie's friends who were all wrapped up in self-image and how many "likes" they got on the latest Instagram post. Katie really wanted to meet Michelle. She appeared genuine to the core and compassionate toward others. What was it about Michelle? Katie wanted to know.

God made us. He already knows everything about us. From knowing our name to knowing the shape of our pinky toe is, God **knows** the details of our lives. But how well do we know Him? Just like Katie, we might sense there is something deeper than just seeing someone from afar. We might have a desire to want to know that person better. The same is true with God. Do you desire a deeper relationship with Him, but don't know where to begin? Psalm 46:10 gives us a great starting point with this Shepherd/ sheep relationship—"Be still, and know that I am God . . . ." This should be the first clue! We tend to be so busy and on-the-go that we don't have the time or take the time to learn more about who God is.

1. Have you ever seen someone from afar and really wanted to meet them? What was it about this person that made you want to get to KNOW them better?

_____

_____

2. How is our relationship with God described in Psalm 100:3? Another word for know is acknowledge. Do you acknowledge God in ALL areas of your life? Why or why not?

_____

_____

3. What does being still mean? What is the opposite of being still? What are practical ways you can be still and acknowledge God to build a stronger relationship with Him?

_____

_____

MORE TO CHEW: We are His SHEEP ~ Psalm 79:13, Ezekiel 34:31, Isaiah 40:11

FLOCK FACTS

SHEEP CANNOT SURVIVE WITHOUT THE PROTECTION OF A SHEPHERD. THEY ARE CREATURES OF HABIT AND WILL NOT MOVE TO AREAS PROVIDING GREENER GRASS ON THEIR OWN. WITH OUT A GOOD SHEPHERD, THEY WILL EAT UNTIL THE GRASS IS GONE AND EVENTUALLY DIE BECAUSE THERE IS NO MORE FOOD.

SHEPHERD'S STAFF

A shepherd's protection is a sheep's main source for survival. As fellow sheep in the care of our Good Shepherd, it is important for us to have survival skills as well. The best survival skill we have is to stay close to our Shepherd. We need to **trust** in His character and love for us. One of the ways we do this is by spending quality time with God. It's called a quiet time. This is a purposeful time set apart from our busy day. Find a cool spot in your house, your favorite couch, or a comfy chair. Light a candle or grab a cool pen. You will need your Bible and maybe a journal to write down your thoughts and prayer concerns. You might take a cool devotional (like this one!) or just read a passage from Scripture. The purpose is to spend time with God intentionally. The more you read the Bible, sit, and be still, the more you will **know** Him personally. It's a promise! Make sure you read "How to have a Quiet Time" in the front of this Bible study. This time with God will never be wasted. It will always be a blessing.

Thank You Lord that I am a sheep in Your pasture, and You are my Good Shepherd. You already know **all** about me. Now it's my turn to know more about YOU. I pray I will find time to spend with You on a daily basis—to be still and know You are God. I pray to meet with You more often and acknowledge who You are in every area of my life. The more I read about You in the Bible, the more I will grow in my relationship with You. I need Your protection. Teach me Your survival skills. This world can be a pretty dangerous place! Amen.

SHEEP ARE NOT SPEEDY

"A truly wise person uses few words;
    a person with understanding is even-tempered.
Even fools are thought wise when they keep silent . . ."

Proverbs 17:27-28 (NLT)

SHEEP'S CORNER

Sheep are not the fastest animals. They don't have speed like a cheetah or even the quick reflexes of a squirrel (who can barely make it across a busy road)! However, sheep can be fast when they need to be—especially when they sense danger. I bet they move their stubby legs pretty fast! For the most part, sheep are laid-back animals. They move at a slow pace.

When you think of the word FAST, what pops into your mind? A sports car? Summer break? A microwave? The first thing that pops into my head is how fast my tongue can get me into trouble. How about you? Have you ever said something you wish you could take back? The Bible has a lot to say about how the **speed** of our speech can get us into dangerous territory. But what about the times when we hold our tongue and don't say what's on our mind? What about when we take our words **slow** . . . like a sheep?

> Samantha was about to tell Annie exactly what was on her mind. Annie was cast as the lead role in the school play, made the junior ballet company, and received an A+ on a very hard science test. Normally Samantha would have been happy for her best friend, but not today. Annie had let all the hoopla go to her head. To put the icing on the cake, she decided not to sit with Samantha at lunch. Annie sat with the cool crowd instead. Sam's feelings were hurt. *"Does Annie think she is better than me?"* Samantha thought to herself. Instead of telling Annie how she really felt, Samantha decided to hold her tongue and give it some time. The next week, Annie did a back handspring and broke her arm. She ended up having surgery and missed the company performance. When Samantha came to her house with flowers, Annie said, "Samantha, I'm sorry I have been such a jerk lately. You are always here for me. Thank you for being my friend."

Not blurting out your feelings is super hard, especially when your feelings are hurt. Proverbs 17:27-28 tells us **we are wise** when we think about our words and hold our tongues—even wiser than getting an A+ on a science test!

1. Read Proverbs 17:27-28. This verse describes someone who controls their tongue. What words are used to describe a wise person?

----

2. What is the result when we STOP to think about our words before we blurt them out?

----

3. Look up James 1:19-20 in your Bible. Why do you think God gave us two ears and one mouth? Why does God call us to be "slow to speak?"

MORE TO CHEW: SPEEDY SPEECH ~ Proverbs 21:23, Proverbs 12:18, 1 Peter 3:10

FLOCK FACTS

SHEPHERDS GO AHEAD OF THE FLOCK TO LOOK OUT FOR POTENTIAL DANGER. WE, TOO, SHOULD LOOK AHEAD TO SEE HOW OUR WORDS CAN EITHER LEAD US INTO SAFE PLACES OR DANGEROUS TERRITORY WHERE FEELINGS CAN GET HURT.

SHEPHERD'S STAFF

Notice how we are identified when we stop to think about how our speech affects others. We are called **wise**, rather than foolish. We are girls with even tempers that have discernment and understanding. We are girls that hold our tongues and not blurt out words we will regret later. Shepherds are always on the lookout for dangerous predators. We, too, should be wise to look ahead and think about where our words will take us. Will our words lead us to dangerous or safe territory? 1 Thessalonians 5:11 says, "Therefore encourage one another and build each other up . . . ." The next time you want to be a speedy sheep, stop and hold your tongue. Don't be like the foolish squirrel darting between quick words only to find yourself under the tire of "I wish I hadn't said that!" Be quick to listen and slow to speak. You will always land safely on the other side.

Father, help me to keep a tight grip on my tongue and take life at a slower pace today. You gave me two ears and one mouth for a reason. I pray I would be wise to listen more and talk less. Give me strength to hold my words even when I don't want to. Help me to build my friends up and not tear them down. Give me **wisdom** today and lead me to safe territory. Thank You for being my Good Shepherd. Amen.

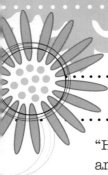

GIVE UP OR PRESS ON?

"He guides the humble in what is right
and teaches them his way.
All the ways of the Lord are loving and faithful
toward those who keep the demands of his covenant."

Psalm 25:9-10

SHEEP'S CORNER

Sheep are pretty much defenseless. They don't have sharp claws like a bear. They can't swim like a duck. They are not camouflaged like a leopard. The best defense sheep have is to stay close to the shepherd—the **good** shepherd. He is good because he loves and takes care of his sheep. He calls them by name and always leads them to safe meadows. I once heard a story about two shepherds and two flocks of sheep. A mighty storm was coming and the shepherds had a decision to make. Would they press on into the storm, or would they form a tight circle and stick it out? One shepherd decided to move ahead, and one decided to stay put. Which flock survived?

Most people don't realize that sheep have **lanolin** in their wool. Lanolin is a waxy layer that serves as a raincoat. It's not waterproof, but it's water resistant. Why is this important? Because the shepherd that took his flock through the storm survived. He took advantage of the lanolin in the sheep's wool to protect them from the rain. Each step forward into the freezing rain was a step toward safe pasture. The lanolin resisted the water and protected the sheep. Unfortunately, the flock that remained tight died. The rain penetrated under the surface of the lanolin and froze their poor bodies.

Connie couldn't believe her situation. Her dance teacher had originally chosen Mary to be the lead in the ballet. However, after Connie made every rehearsal and put forth great effort, the dance teacher decided to give Connie the lead and move Mary to under study. This was not good. This was not good **at all**. The word spread quickly. A rumor spread that Connie's mom had paid her dance teacher to give her the lead. Connie was devastated. She wanted to work hard and be the best ballerina she could be, but NOT at the expense of gossip and lies. She wanted to quit and give up.
With the advice from her mom, she decided to **press on** through this storm and **trust** that God would lead her into what was right and good.

The surviving sheep and Connie have something in common. Because they walked forward in the storm and didn't give up, the rain of disappointing circumstances never got the best of them. They pressed on in difficult times and into safe pasture.

1. Are you going through a storm right now? Sheep have lanolin to protect them in the storm. What do we have that gives us the courage to press on?

- -

2. Just as wool resists rain, how can we resist hurtful comments, unfair circumstances, and broken dreams?

- -

3. What are specific actions we can take to step forward and trust where the Good Shepherd leads? How is Psalm 25:9-10 a comfort in the storms of life?

- -

- -

MORE TO CHEW: PRESSING ON ~ Romans 8:28, 2 Corinthians 12:10, Philippians 3:14

SHEPHERD'S STAFF

FLOCK FACTS

LANOLIN IS THE WAXY RESIDUE LEFT AFTER SHEEP'S WOOL IS BOILED, COOLED, AND PRESSED THROUGH CHEESE CLOTH IT WAS SHEPHERD'S CHAP-STICK IN THE FIRST CENTURY. TODAY, LIPSTICKS, MASCARA, LOTIONS, AND SHAMPOOS CONTAIN LANOLIN.

God will always lead us in the right direction, especially when we see freezing rain storms ahead! We cannot stop or give up in hard times. (Although it's super easy, right?) Psalm 25:9-10 tells us that ALL the ways of the Lord are loving and faithful. When we follow the Good Shepherd, He gives us lanolin, too. He provides the resistance we need when hurtful comments, broken dreams, past mistakes, or team losses want to saturate our thoughts and penetrate our souls. Hard situations can be like freezing rain. If we don't put on the raincoat of God's protection, disappointments will paralyze us. Instead of giving up and quitting, **trust** in God's direction and use these situations to make you stronger. Don't quit. Keep moving. Take advantage of your "lanolin" and trust God to use your circumstances for His purposes.

Father, it's hard to walk through the storms of life. It's hard not to give up when life seems unfair. Teach me to trust You in these times and to believe that Your ways are always right. You will never lead me into dangerous situations. Help me to take advantage of Your protection, Your strength, and Your love. The next time I hit a storm of disappointment, help me to walk through it with confidence. You are my Good Shepherd! Amen.

ART PROJECT: HE KNOWS MY NAME JOURNAL

ART SUPPLIES

- Composition Notebook
- Scrapbook Paper
- Optional: Wallpaper samples
- Elmer's Glue and Glue Sticks
- Foam Brushes
- White Pipe Cleaners
- Scissors
- Pencil
- Buttons
- Sheep and Scripture Template
- Credit Card/ Hotel Card
- Optional: Low-Temp Glue Gun/Glue

• All templates can be found on www.thouartexalted.com under the He Knows My Name 20/20 Mini tab.

HE KNOWS MY NAME.

"HE CALLS HIS OWN SHEEP BY NAME

AND LEADS THEM OUT" JN 10:3

INSTRUCTIONS:

TIPS:
- Notebooks are $1 at Dollar Tree.
- When gluing paper to notebook, don't use too much glue. If the paper starts to "bubble," use an old credit card or hotel key card to smooth out the paper.
- Templates are found under the He Knows My Name Bible Study for Girls tab on www.thouartexalted.com
- Wallpaper samples will cover the notebook front to back.

1. Open your composition notebook. Lay it on the back side of your scrapbook paper or wallpaper. Using a pencil, trace around the notebook and cut. Using a foam brush, glue paper to the outside of your notebook. (See **tip** on "bubbling.")

2. After covering the front and back, cut a strip of coordinating paper (2" x 9.75") and glue as a "binder" that covers 3/4 of an inch on front and back. Optional: For a clean look, glue the first page of notebook paper to the inside and back cover.

3. Download the templates. Trace the sheep shapes onto your paper. Cut and glue.

4. For the final touches, glue buttons, sequins, pipe cleaner clouds, and add the Scripture.

"I love to write in my journal because it's my go to. I am always encouraged to see where God is working in my life." - Isabel (7th grade)

HE KNOWS MY NAME.

"HE CALLS HIS OWN SHEEP BY NAME

AND LEADS THEM

SHEEP CANNOT DOG PADDLE

"The Lord is my shepherd, I shall not want.
He makes me lie down in green pastures;
He leads me beside quiet waters."

Psalm 23:1-2 (NASB)

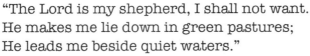

SHEEP'S CORNER

Did you know that sheep cannot swim? If they fall into a rapidly moving river, their wool will quickly absorb water and add weight to their bodies. The chances for survival are slim because sheep cannot dog paddle, much less do the freestyle. The good news is that sheep are generally afraid of quick-moving streams. A good shepherd will go ahead of his flock to make sure the stream is a safe, quiet, and peaceful place for them to drink. Today we are looking at one of the most famous Psalms in the Bible, Psalm 23. The first two verses make it very clear that God is our Good Shepherd who provides what we need, but not always what we want. Notice where He leads us—to **quiet** waters. Do you suppose God knows when the roaring waters of crazy circumstances can be too much for us?

> Christy was beyond excited that she had been invited to the party. She always felt like this group was too cool for her, but not this time! She was finally considered popular enough to be invited to Kaylee's birthday party. She spent hours choosing the right outfit and even watched some videos online for how to braid her hair. She wanted to look perfect. When she got to the party, she didn't see any of her friends and started to feel a little out of place. No worries. Kaylee came to her side as everyone gathered around to play the game of truth or dare. At first it wasn't so bad, until they dared Christy to kiss the boy to her right. Her heart sank. Never ever would she do such a thing. She felt like she was way over her head and was drowning by the second. Just as she was feeling sick to her stomach, Kaylee's mom announced it was time for snacks and cake. Whew. That was way too close for Christy. She called her mom to come and pick her up. Being popular was not worth the time or the stomach ache.

The river of popularity was faster than Christy imagined! She thought she "wanted" to be included in the cool crowd, but once she accepted the invitation, she realized the waters were too deep for her to swim. Psalm 23:1-2 says the Good Shepherd will only lead us to quiet waters, not dangerous waters where our safety is in jeopardy. The Good Shepherd **always** has us in His care and **always** leads us to places that provide peace rather than harm. The word "quiet" means a place of rest, to rest, or a quiet place. Christy knew in her heart that the waters of her circumstances were way over her head. She was drowning and longed for the Good Shepherd to rescue her.

16.

1. Have you ever been in a situation that looked exciting, only to realize that you were way over your head? Who did you turn to for rescue?

---

2. Psalm 23:1 says, "I shall not want." Why do you think the Good Shepherd gives us what we need and not what we want?

---

3. Why do you think the Good Shepherd leads us to quiet waters and not rushing waters?

MORE TO CHEW: God provides our needs ~ Philippians 4:19, James 4:1-2, Romans 8:32

SHEPHERD'S STAFF

FLOCK FACTS

DID YOU KNOW THAT SHEEP ARE INSTINCTIVELY AFRAID OF RUSHING WATERS? NO MATTER HOW THIRSTY THEY ARE, THEY WILL NOT DRINK FROM RAPID WATERS. THE GOOD SHEPHERD WILL OFTEN GO UPSTREAM TO LAY DOWN ROCKS MAKING THE STREAM "QUIET" FOR HIS SHEEP TO DRINK.

A good shepherd knows that sheep will drown in deep water. God knows this, too. He knows exactly what we need and protects us from the roaring waters of dangerous circumstances by leading us to still waters. But like sheep, we tend to wander away from the Good Shepherd's protection and go our own way. Isaiah 53:6 says, "All of us, like sheep, have strayed away. We have left God's paths to follow our own . . . ." Sometimes we want something so badly, we jump into deep waters without thinking things through, just like Christy. We find ourselves catching our breath and longing for the Good Shepherd to rescue us. The good news is God is always there to **protect** us. The next time you are tempted to jump into an unknown situation, ask the Good Shepherd if the water is too deep. Trust Him and follow His leading.

Thank You Lord that You will never lead me where the water is too deep. You are my Good Shepherd who gives me only what I need and not what I want. This can be really hard sometimes because I want a lot of things. But only You know what is good for me. You know what is too deep for me to handle. Lead me into safe pasture and quiet waters where I can be content and satisfied. Teach me to trust in You and follow Your lead. Amen.

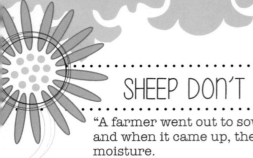

SHEEP DON'T HAVE SOCIAL CALENDARS

"A farmer went out to sow his seed. . . . Some fell on rocky ground, and when it came up, the plants withered because they had no moisture. Luke 8:5-6

"The seeds in the gravel are those who hear with enthusiasm, but the enthusiasm doesn't go very deep. It's only another fad, and the moment there's trouble it's gone. Luke 8:13 (MSG)

SHEEP'S CORNER

Sheep don't have much on their social calendars. They don't have errands to run, chores to do, or parties to attend. They don't have cell phones, Facebook, or Instagram. They can't tweet. In fact, they just eat. And eat. And eat. On the other hand, we are busy all the time! Think about **all** you do during the day. The minute you wake up you jump into breakfast, school, tests, friends, a little drama, and then leap into afternoon activities like ballet, gymnastics, soccer, volleyball, piano, or youth group. With a quick bite and maybe a "hello" to Mom, you are off to study or do homework just to repeat the cycle again! While sheep do not have the busy schedule you have, you do have one thing in common—**water**. Water is the most important nutrient we need to stay hydrated. Without water, we can't keep up with all the day's activities.

Joani was excited about **all** the activities she had planned for the weekend. Her best friend, Anna, was coming to town! Anna was coming to school with Joani on Friday followed by dinner and the football game. Saturday morning they were planning to cook their favorite breakfast and then head to the Town Center. Joani was excited to get her ears pierced, and she was waiting for Anna to be there with her. After buying some new earrings they would meet up with some of Joani's friends, walk around, shop, and end up at Joani's house for a slumber party. Her plans were running smoothly until Joani felt light headed after she got her ears pierced. Walking in the hot sun, Joani began to feel dizzy. With all the excitement, Joani forgot to drink water all morning and afternoon. She grabbed Anna's hand and fainted in her arms.

Did you know that girls need to drink about 8 cups of water a day? Sheep need about 2 gallons of water a day! Because the human body is made up of (on average) 60% water, we need to replenish on a daily basis. Luke 8 talks about a different kind of water that is just as important—maybe not for sheep, but definitely for girls with busy schedules. Just as we need water to keep us physically healthy, we need the Living Water of God's Word to keep us spiritually healthy.

1. Have you ever been dehydrated and felt dizzy? What happens when we do not drink enough water?

----

2. In The Parable of the Sower, the farmer is God, and the seed is the Word of God. Why did the plant wither in Luke 8:5-6? Why is water important for a seed to grow?

----

3. Jesus tells us in Luke 8:13 that some people hear God's Word and are super excited, but when trouble comes, that enthusiasm goes away. Why do you think this happens?

MORE TO CHEW: The Living Water ~ John 7:37–39, Ephesians 1:13–14, John 14:26

FLOCK FACTS

DID YOU KNOW THAT SHEEP WILL DRINK FROM 1.2 TO 4 GALLONS OF WATER A DAY? THEY CAN GET MOST OF THEIR WATER INTAKE FROM THE WATER IN THE GRASS, BUT WHEN THEY EAT HAY, THEY GET MORE THIRSTY. SHEEP ALSO DO NOT LIKE TO DRINK DIRTY WATER.

SHEPHERD'S STAFF

A good shepherd always makes sure his flock gets plenty of water. We, too, need plenty of water—physical and Living Water. The Bible tells us the Living Water is the Holy Spirit. When we believe in Jesus, the Holy Spirit comes and lives in us! The Holy Spirit is our teacher and guide, and He will remind us of what we have learned in the Bible. Jesus tells us that the seed, God's Word planted in our hearts, needs to get lots of water. Why? Because trouble and hardship will dehydrate our faith. Our enthusiasm for Christianity withers and we begin to question if Jesus is really our Good Shepherd. In times like these, we need to drink more water to deepen our faith. There is a reason why a good shepherd leads his sheep to quiet waters and not BUSY waters. Our quiet waters are called "quiet" times with God to refresh, restart, and rest. This Living Water gives us the courage to press on. Don't get dehydrated when trouble comes. The Living Water, the Holy Spirit, will deepen your roots and water the seed of God's Word in your heart!

I thank You Lord that You have given me life on this earth! You have given me a brain to think, arms to swim, legs to run, and a heart to love. You have also given me the Holy Spirit to strengthen me when times are hard. The Holy Spirit reminds me of Your truths when I am feeling weak. Just like water strengthens my body when I am dehydrated, Your Living Water provides the hope I need when I am faced with difficult situations. I pray to be quiet with You this week and fill up in the presence of the Living Water. Amen.

FOLLOW THE LEADER

"I cry aloud to the Lord; I lift up my voice to the Lord for mercy. I pour out before him my complaint; before him I tell my trouble. When my spirit grows faint within me, it is you who know my way."

Psalm 142:1-3

SHEEP'S CORNER

A good shepherd watches his sheep at **all** times. In fact, we read in Luke chapter two that while the shepherds were living out in the fields and keeping watch over their flocks at night, the angel of the Lord appeared to them to tell them about the birth of baby Jesus. This verse tells us three important characteristics about shepherds. They **live** with the sheep, they are **awake** even at night, and they keep **watch** at all times. Live. Awake. Watch. Shepherds are always taking care of and protecting their sheep. Why? Because they **know** them. They know their names. They know what food they like to eat. They know what makes their tummies hurt. They know if they are injured. They know if they are thirsty. They know if they are in trouble. And shepherds **know** the way that is best for them.

> Mandy's Journal: I am not sure I can handle the pressure anymore. I feel so overwhelmed. It's hard to balance school, homework, and sports—not to mention the drama with my friends. My parents are fighting again, and my mom had to get a new job to help with the finances. I have more responsibility at home now, and I am not sure I can handle it all. I used to be so happy and bright. Now I feel like I am angry all the time. I am trying to appear like everything is OK on the outside, but on the inside I feel like I am barely shining. Help me, Lord. You know my situation, and You know my way. I need Your protection and direction. I just don't feel like me anymore.
>
> ~ MANDY

Do you ever feel like Mandy? Have you ever felt like you are drowning in responsibility and overwhelmed by the circumstances in your life? Here is good news. The Good Shepherd, Jesus, is watching over you just as shepherds watch over their sheep. At night, during the day, when you are sleeping, dealing with girl drama, playing your game, while studying for a test . . . Jesus is always there. Psalm 142:3 also reminds us that Jesus **knows our way**. He knows when we are struggling and when we are overwhelmed by life's circumstances. His suggestion? Talk to Him. Take some advice from King David (who wrote this psalm btw). Cry out to Him. Lift up your voice to Him. Pour out your complaints to Him. Tell Him your troubles. And when you feel like your spirit is growing faint, put your trust in Him. He knows the way.

1. What circumstances in your life seem to be overwhelming? When do you feel like your spirit grows "faint" within you?

----

2. What do you do when you feel overwhelmed? Who do you turn to? What are the four actions Psalm 142:1-3 tells us to take?

----

3. Read Isaiah 41:10. How do we know God is watching over us and is always with us? What three things will He do for us?

MORE TO CHEW: God KNOWS our way ~ John 10:3, Proverbs 3:5-6, John 14:1,6

SHEPHERD'S STAFF

FLOCK FACTS

A SHEPHERD WILL STAY AWAKE ALL NIGHT WHEN PREDATORS ARE MORE LIKELY TO ATTACK. DID YOU KNOW GOD NEVER SLEEPS EITHER? PSALM 121:4 SAYS "HE WHO WATCHES OVER ISRAEL WILL NEITHER SLUMBER NOR SLEEP. GOD IS OUR TRUE GOOD SHEPHERD!

God knows our way. Everyday He is leading us into new pastures. Yes, life can be overwhelming, but instead of focusing on your circumstance, **follow the leader**—and trust in the Good Shepherd who knows the way. Follow the instructions from the psalmist and cry out to the Lord. Lift up your voice and pour out your heart. It feels great to pray aloud and release the pressures from within. Try it! Pray this prayer with some voice! "God, here is my situation: I feel overwhelmed by _____, and _____, and _____. I know You are my Good Shepherd, and You are my strength. I trust in You! Come and help me. You know the way." Psalm 16:8 tells us to set the Lord always before us because He is at our right hand. No matter how faint your spirit, focus on Jesus. He is your sustainer and protector. Set Him before you and not your situation. And don't forget to pray out loud!

You are always watching me and know the best direction for me. Even when life seems too much for me to handle, You know the way. I place my trust in You. I will set my focus on You and NOT on the circumstances that are overwhelming me. Jesus, go before me today. You are my strength in weakness. You will never leave my side. You know the way. I will follow the leader. Amen.

PACMAN POWER

"No one has ever seen God; but if we love one another, God lives in us and his love is made complete in us."

1 John 4:12

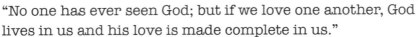
SHEEP'S CORNER

No one has ever seen God, but 1 John 4:12 tells us that when we love others people will **see** God through our actions. How can this be—especially when it's hard to love? It's easy to love someone when they are nice, generous, kind, and compassionate. Think about your friends. Why is it easy to love them? Are they fun? Do they find the good and positive in a situation? Are they creative? Encouraging? Smart? Energetic? But what about loving people who are annoying, grumpy, and are always complaining? It is not as easy to love someone who gets on your nerves, who is unfriendly, mean, or who has done something to hurt you.

Amber had enough of her brother Jake. Jake was always going into her room without permission. This time, he went too far. Jake found Amber's diary and read through ALL of it. If that wasn't enough, Jake told his friends about Amber's crush at school. When Amber's friends heard about it, they started teasing her. After school, Amber ran into her room crying and locked the door. "Who cares anyway? I hate Jake for what he did to me," she mumbled through her tears. That night, Amber prayed before she went to bed. *"Dear Lord, I know it's hard to love people when they have hurt you, especially my brother. This is a really hard prayer, Lord. I don't even like him right now. Please help me to forgive him for what he has done to me. Amen."*

Have you ever heard the phrase, "Every flock has a black sheep?" A black sheep is someone who may be hard to love. God is not asking us to be best friends with everyone, but He is telling us to love one another. Why? Because when we do, people can **see** God. Thank goodness God gives us **help** to love others. This helper is called the Holy Spirit. Have you ever played the video game Pac-Man? Have you ever noticed that Pac-Man gets supernatural power and turns blue when he eats the cherries? This fruit-filled power gives him the ability to destroy the ghosts. The same is true with the Holy Spirit. When we accept Jesus, the Holy Spirit gives us power, too. When we choose to love one another, we are filled with God's power to do the impossible, like forgiving our brothers. Be filled with God's power and eat some cherries, God's fruitful power booster. Love one another so others can see God in you and destroy the ghosts. Don't worry, you won't turn blue, but you will shine!

1. Name someone that is easy for you to love. What is it about them that is easy to love?

_____

_____

2. When has it been hard for you to love someone? How can you use the power of the Holy Spirit to help you?

_____

_____

3. Read Galatians 5:22-23. What are the fruits of the Spirit? What specific fruit do you need today to show God's love?

_____

_____

_____

MORE TO CHEW: Holy Spirit empowers us ~ John 14:26, Romans 8:26, John 14:15-17

SHEPHERD'S STAFF

FLOCK FACTS

DID YOU KNOW THAT BLACK SHEEP WERE CONSIDERED NOT AS VALUABLE AS WHITE SHEEP BECAUSE THEIR WOOL COULD NOT BE DYED? BUT ACCORDING TO LEGEND, ONE BLACK SHEEP IN A FLOCK WAS CONSIDERED GOOD LUCK BY SHEPHERDS!

Look at the fruit of the Spirit (love, joy, peace, patience, kindness, goodness, faithfulness, gentleness, and self-control) and think about their opposites. What is the opposite of love? Hate. What about patience? Impatience. What about gentleness? Pushy. Abrasive. Rude. These are the ghosts that keep us from loving one another. They also stop us from seeing God. This is exactly why we need the power of the Holy Spirit to empower us. When we accept Jesus, the Holy Spirit lives in us. The question is not whether He is present, but whether we will allow Him to work. Just as a shepherd is always there to guide his flock, God is always there to guide us, too. God will never leave us to love on our own. The Holy Spirit will teach us and show us what fruit we need in each situation. Although we can't see Him, others can see God in us when we choose to be empowered (eat some holy cherries) and power up the Holy Spirit in our lives!

Lord, thank You for the power of the Holy Spirit. I pray others will see You in me when I activate the fruit and munch on some impatience, rudeness, and downright bad attitudes. I pray You will guide me to love, peace, and joy. I pray You will show me how to love especially when it's hard. Thank You that You will never leave me and will always lead me in the right direction. May Your love be complete in me today. Amen.

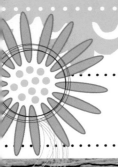

ART PROJECT:
PSALM 23 • SHEEP CANVAS

ART SUPPLIES

- 6 x 6 Gallery Wrap Canvas
- Acrylic Paints: (mustard yellow, green, lime green, blue, black, white)
- Elmer's Glue
- Scrapbook Paper
- Pencil
- Template (www.thouartexalted.com)
- Scripture
- Plastic Knife
- Plastic Plate
- Paper Towels
- Scissors
- Straw Hay (Tip: Dollar Tree)
- Embellishments: (sequins, paper flowers, buttons, etc.)

"The Lord is my shepherd; I have all that I need. He lets me rest in green meadows; he leads me beside peaceful streams. He renews my strength. He guides me along right paths." Psalm 23:1-3

INSTRUCTIONS:

1. Paint your 6 x 6 canvas black. Let dry. Squirt three colors onto your plastic plate: blue, green, and a mustard yellow. Visually, divide your canvas into three sections: sky, water, and grass. Using your plastic knife (as a palate knife), scoop the color onto your knife and scrape it onto your canvas. Be generous with the color but don't over paint the canvas. You will want the black to show through. Let dry.

2. While paint is drying, print out Scripture and template from www.thouartexalted.com. Cut out sheep form, sheep head, and Scripture. Pick out fun scrapbook paper for the head of your sheep. Trace and cut out.

3. Using a pencil, lightly trace the body form onto your canvas. Using white paint and your palate knife, paint the body onto the canvas. Pull down extra white paint to add sheep legs.

4. Once canvas is dry, embellish your art with the Scripture, beads, pebbles, paper flowers, and sequins. Make sure you sign your art and always remember, you have a Good Shepherd who is looking out for you!

"This art reminds me that God will give me what I need, not necessarily what I want. And, that's always better!"
– Maddie (8th grade)

"The Lord is my shepherd; I have all that I need. He lets me rest in green meadows; he leads me beside peaceful streams. He renews my strength. He guides me along right paths." Psalm 23:1-3

FLIPPED OVER

"Turn your ear to me, come quickly to my rescue; be my rock of refuge, a strong fortress to save me. Since you are my rock and my fortress, for the sake of your name lead me and guide me."

Psalm 31:2,3

When sheep flip over on their backs, it is very hard for them to flip back over without the help of the good shepherd. If a sheep flips over in shallow waters, it can drown simply because it cannot get back up! This is another reason why it's so important for the shepherd to be constantly watching over his flock with care. It is interesting that the word "to flip over" can also mean "to be cast out." We see this in the story where Jesus heals a man born blind in John chapter 9. (It's a little long, but worth reading!) The teachers of that day were furious at Jesus for healing a blind man on the Sabbath, the day of rest. In fact, they were so mad they "cast" or kicked the man out of the synagogue! In a sense, they flipped the healed blind man over on the most exciting day of his life. Who would be there to rescue him?

Lucy was jumping for joy that she had been awarded Most Valuable Player (MVP) for middle school softball as catcher. She deserved it, too! For the past two seasons, she was admitted to the hospital for concussions. But this year was different. The only problem with taking this position meant replacing her best friend, Tammy, as catcher. There was definite conflict, and Lucy could feel it. Tammy was jealous and mad that Lucy had gotten the award. In her anger, Tammy refused to talk to Lucy and even made plans to exclude her from her birthday party. Lucy's excitement was drowned by frustration and confusion. Shouldn't Tammy be proud of Lucy for persevering and getting the award? Lucy felt like their friendship had been flipped over.

If we continue to read the story of the healed blind man, we see that when Jesus heard he was thrown out, he went and **found** him. He asked him, "Do you believe in the son of man?" The man replied, "Lord, I believe" (John 9:35-38). Jesus didn't waste any time to find the healed blind man and flip him back over. Jesus knew this man had been cast out and flipped over by jealousy and anger—just like Lucy. Psalm 31:2,3 tells us that God is our rock and our refuge. He hears us when we cry out to Him and will come to our rescue. He knows when one of His beloved sheep gets flipped over. Jesus is always right there to stand us on our two feet.

1. Have you ever been in a situation where you felt cast out or flipped over? Who came to your rescue? Do you cry out to God when you need to be rescued? Why or why not?

_____

_____

2. What do you think is the definition of rock, strength, and refuge? Read Psalm 31:2,3. Why do you think God is described as our rock of refuge and our strong fortress?

_____

_____

3. Jesus asked the healed blind man a very important question. "Do you BELIEVE in the son of man?" How does belief in Jesus allow us to be rescued by Him?

_____

_____

_____

MORE TO CHEW: Jesus is Our Rescue ~ Psalm 91:14, Colossians 1:13, Galatians 1:4

SHEPHERD'S STAFF

FLOCK FACTS

DID YOU KNOW THAT A SHEPHERD WILL RISK HIS OWN LIFE TO RESCUE ONE OF HIS SHEEP? HE TAKES HIS JOB VERY SERIOUSLY. SHEEP DEPEND ON THEIR SHEPHERD FOR PROTECTION, AND A GOOD SHEPHERD WILL DO WHATEVER IT TAKES TO DEFEND A SHEEP AGAINST A PREDATOR.

Our belief in Jesus plays a key role in our rescue. Why? When we believe Jesus is the Son of God and we believe He came to rescue us from our sins, we trust in Him to lead us and be our guide through life. We **know** He is our Good Shepherd. We **know** He hears us when we pray. We **know** He is our strong refuge in times of trouble. Psalm 91:14,15 says, "'Because he loves me,' says the Lord, 'I will rescue Him; I will protect him, for he acknowledges my name. He will call upon me, and I will answer; I will be with him in trouble. . . .'" Wow. What a promise! We always have a Good Shepherd who will flip us back over when we are flipped over. We should do the same. When you see your friends or family that have been flipped over, encourage them with some good advice from the Shepherd. Find them right away in their sorrow and love on them. Show them you care and guide them to Jesus.

Thank You Lord that You are right there for me when I am flipped over by hurtful comments, broken relationships, disappointment, and despair. Thank You that You do not leave me alone in my trouble. You listen to my prayers. You guide me through spending time with You and reading Your Word. You lead me through the encouragement and fellowship of other believers. You will protect me for You are my Good Shepherd. Today, I acknowledge Your name. Help me be a fellow "flipper-back-over" and encourage other sheep to follow You. Amen.

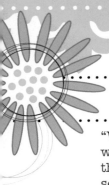

THE WEAK WILL BECOME STRONG

"When the angel of the Lord appeared to Gideon, he said, 'The Lord is with you, **mighty warrior**.' . . . The Lord turned to him and said, 'Go in the strength you have and save Israel out of Midian's hand. Am I not sending you?' 'Pardon me, my lord,' Gideon replied, 'but how can I save Israel? My clan is the weakest in Manasseh, and I am the least in my family.'"

Judges 6:12-15

SHEEP'S CORNER

Sheep are considered weak animals because they cannot protect themselves. They are skittish and slow. Sheep eat all day, and they do not have the highest intellect. Sorry little sheep! In the line up with the lion, the bear, and the cheetah, the sheep fall in last place. This is another reason why a shepherd's care is most important. Where we are weak, He is strong! Today, we are looking at the story of Gideon in the Old Testament. When the angel of the Lord appeared to him, Gideon was hiding from the Midianites who were trying to destroy their land. I imagine when the angel looked at Gideon and said, "The Lord is with you, mighty warrior," he might have looked over his shoulder to see if the angel was talking to someone else. He sure didn't see himself as mighty. After all, he was hiding from the enemy. Who was mighty? Not Gideon. He considered himself the weakest of the weak.

Charlotte didn't see herself as being creative at all. In fact, her first grade teacher told her she didn't have a creative bone in her body. Of course, Charlotte was devastated and promised never picked up a paint brush again. When she was sixteen, Charlotte had to take an art class to graduate from high school, and Exploring Watercolor 101 was the only elective. Who was she to take a watercolor class? She hid in the back of the class when an energetic and enthusiastic teacher said, "Greetings, future artists!" Charlotte looked around the room and wanted to run for her life. Why was this teacher calling her an artist? Clearly she did not know that Charlotte was the furthest thing from artistic. By the end of the year, Charlotte's paintings were the talk of the school. Not only did she win the most improved artist, but she received an art scholarship to the local university. "*Crazy,*" she thought to herself, "*Just when I wanted to hide, my creativity was there all the time!*"

Gideon and Charlotte have a lot in common—they were both hiding from what they thought was a weakness. Gideon thought he was too weak to be a warrior and fight for Israel. Charlotte thought she was uncreative and hid from her art teacher. Both of them had a future strength only God could see. Both needed the guidance of the Good Shepherd **to lead** them into their strengths when they would have been very happy to stay right where they were, in hiding.

1. Has God ever surprised you with a hidden talent or the strength to do something that you thought you could never do? Explain.

_____

_____

2. What are areas in your life where you feel weak? Eating sweets? Controlling your tongue? Your temper? Your self image? Comparing yourself to others? Why?

_____

_____

3. The Lord promised Gideon to "Go in the strength you have . . . Am I (the LORD) not sending you?" How can we overcome our weaknesses and trust in God's strength?

_____

_____

_____

MORE TO CHEW: Jesus is our Strength ~ Philippians 4:13, Isaiah 40:29, Ephesians 6:10

SHEPHERD'S STAFF

FLOCK FACTS

SHEPHERDS ARE CALLED TO STRENGTHEN THE SHEEP WHEN THEY ARE WEAK. THEY WILL BANDAGE THE HURT, HEAL THE DISEASED, LEAD THE HUNGRY TO SAFE PASTURE, AND PROTECT THE DEFENSELESS FROM PREDATORS. WE CANNOT BE MADE STRONGER WITHOUT THE HELP OF A GOOD SHEPHERD.

Do you remember the old song, Jesus loves me? *Jesus loves me, this I know. For the Bible tells me so. Little ones to Him belong. They are weak but He is STRONG!* Just like sheep, we, too, are weak. But just like Gideon, we can be strong. God sees a **mighty warrior** in all of us to go and do the things He has gifted us to do. Jesus is our Good Shepherd, and He is our strength. We cannot depend on our own strength because it won't last very long. Take courage in these verses. Philippians 4:13 says, "I can do ALL things through Christ who strengthens me." Isaiah 40:31 says, "But those who hope in the LORD will renew their strength. They will soar on wings like eagles; they will run and not grow weary, they will walk and not be faint." 2 Corinthians 12:9-10 says, "My grace is sufficient for you, for my power is made perfect in weakness." God often sees what we cannot. He sees a brave and strong warrior. Do not be afraid and step out into the strength of the Lord today.

Lord, You are my strength when I am weak. I have to admit that when I am scared to try something new or step out into the unknown, I am hesitant. Remind me to sing that Jesus loves me and when I am weak, He is strong. I know You can use me even when I am afraid. Teach me to be like Gideon. Teach me to trust in Your strength and not my own. Help me to step out in faith. I want to be like the eagle. I want to soar and not grow faint. I want to see my weakness made perfect in Your power. Amen.

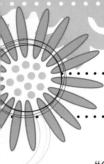

SHEEP ARE NEAR-SIGHTED

"Open my eyes to see the wonderful things in your law."
Psalm 119:18

SHEEP'S CORNER

Sheep have trouble with depth perception. In fact, some experts say sheep are near-sighted. The combination of these two visual handicaps puts sheep in a vulnerable position. Depth perception is not being able to tell the distance of a far away object. Near-sighted means you can see an object more clearly that is closer than an object that is far away. Believe me, I know! I am legally blind. When I take off my glasses at night, I can't see a thing. Every object is super blurry. Thank goodness I can wear glasses so I can see clearly, but what about sheep? Poor depth perception plus near-sightedness are two strikes against you when a predator is sneaking up to eat you. Hmmm? Is that a rock or a cougar? We need to have clear vision, too. We need to **trust** in the Good Shepherd who knows what's in front of us, what's behind us, and who's in the bushes.

> Hannah was trying extra hard to focus on what Mr. Bell was writing on the white board. She had a science test tomorrow and needed to write everything down perfectly in her notebook. That's when she started to get a headache and all the words seemed to blur into one another. Mr. Bell saw her squinting and asked if she could see the board clearly. Admitting that the words were blurry, he suggested that Hannah get an appointment to get her eyes checked. Hannah was so relieved when the doctor put glasses on her eyes. Wow! Had the world been this clear before? Hannah had a new lease on life. She had no idea how blurry things had been.

Think about all the things you could not do if you couldn't see clearly. What about playing sports, reading the white board, or seeing expressions on people's faces? The God's Word translation of Psalm 119:18 says, "Uncover my eyes so that I may see the miraculous things in your teachings." The Psalmist is teaching us a prayer we should pray every morning before our feet touch the floor. To uncover means to reveal, to bring to light, or to expose. Mr. Bell uncovered or revealed to Hannah the truth that she needed to get her eyes checked. God also will uncover and reveal the truth of His Word when we are willing to ask. We will not always know why God allows hardship into our lives, but we can always trust in His **supernatural vision**. He can see things we cannot.

1. Do you have poor eyesight or know someone who does? How does this limit your/their vision?

----

2. Read Psalm 119:18. The New Living Translation reads, "Open my eyes to see the wonderful truths in your instructions." What are these wonderful things or truths?

----

3. Does a situation in your life seem blurry? How can focusing on the wonderful things in God's instruction clear your vision?

MORE TO CHEW: Pay Attention to God~Hebrews 2:1, Luke 8:18, Proverbs 3:21, Psalm 91:14

SHEPHERD'S STAFF

FLOCK FACTS

WHILE SHEEP HAVE POOR DEPTH PERCEPTION AND CAN'T SEE OBJECTS CLEARLY THAT ARE FAR AWAY, THEY HAVE GREAT PERIPHERAL VISION. THEY CAN EVEN SEE BEHIND THEM WITHOUT MOVING THEIR HEADS! THAT WOULD BE A GREAT TRICK TO TAKE TO A PARTY!

Vision is one of our five senses, but often we do not see things clearly. We can get so focused on what is right under our noses that we can't see the bigger picture. The center of our attention starts revolving around our circumstances and before we know it, our vision of what God is doing in our lives is blurred. When life gets tough and circumstances seem to be the central focus, ask God to open your eyes to see what Jesus, the Good Shepherd, is doing. Ask Him to reveal His wonderful truths into your heart. When your vision becomes unclear and the predators of discouragement, worry, stress, and bitterness seem to leap out of the bushes, call on the Good Shepherd. Ask Him to reveal His promises to you. God's Word tells to be aware, pay attention, and stay focused on the wisdom and understanding of God's law. The Good Shepherd is always there to uncover His good plans for us.

Lord, You can see far into the distance of my life with a clarity I cannot. I guess this teaches me to trust You even more. I know You can see from a viewpoint I cannot. You also have a perspective on my life I cannot see either. You promise me Your plans are good, and I believe in that promise today. When I tend to focus on the immediate circumstance and begin to feel blurred with emotion, help me to open my eyes to Your wonderful things. I am thankful for Your supernatural vision and life perception. Amen.

SHEEP KNOW THE SHEPHERD'S VOICE

"After he has gathered his own flock, he walks ahead of them, and they follow him because they know his voice."

John 10:4 (NLT)

SHEEP'S CORNER

When a shepherd calls his sheep, they follow. John 10:4 tells us that the reason they follow is because they know his **voice**. It's very interesting to look at the order in which the shepherd gathers his flock. First, he brings them out. Then, he walks ahead of them. Finally, he calls them to follow His lead. He is the leader of the flock, and the sheep follow because they trust him and know him. The word "know" means to discern, to see, or to examine. These sheep discern his voice because they remember where he has led them before—to safe pastures. Their commitment to the shepherd is evident. Their faith is deep. They will not follow anyone else. They are a loyal flock.

> Bridget had a big decision to make. The exciting news was that she was offered a volleyball scholarship. The not so exciting news was that she would have to transfer schools to take the offer. She loved her old school and her friends. It was true the scholarship would help her family's finances since her dad had lost his job. But what about Bridget? Was money the only reason she would make this huge leap? One voice was telling her to stay at her old school and not change a thing. The other voice was telling her to take a chance and trust in this fantastic opportunity. She loved volleyball, she wanted to help her parents, and she respected the new coach. Which voice should she listen to?

The voices we listen to are very important as they have the power to direct our lives. And, believe me, there are many voices to which we can listen! We can listen to the voice of temptation, the voice of peer pressure, or the voice of popularity. We can listen to the voice of selfishness, the voice of pride, or the voice of insecurity. We can also listen to the voice of reason, the voice of truth, or the voice of faith. It's our decision who we follow. It's also our decision which voice we listen to. As the shepherd goes ahead of the flock, Jesus goes ahead of us, too. A good question to ask when you are discerning between voices is this: Where is the voice leading me? If it leads you to the fruits of the spirit—love, joy, peace, patience, kindness, goodness, etc—that's the voice to follow. If sheep can discern, examine, and follow the voice of the Good Shepherd, so can we!

1. How can you tell the difference between what you want to do and what the Good Shepherd wants you to do? What are some practical ways to listen for God's voice?

2. Why do you think the shepherd walks ahead of the flock before he calls them? How does this make a difference in your decisions knowing Jesus walks ahead of you?

3. Deuteronomy 1:30 says "God goes before you and will fight for you. . . ." How does this verse give you encouragement as you discern the Good Shepherd's voice?

MORE TO CHEW: God Goes Ahead~Deuteronomy 1:30, Deuteronomy 31:8, Isaiah 52:12

FLOCK FACTS

DID YOU KNOW THAT ANOTHER WORD FOR STEADFAST FAITH IS ALSO KNOWN AS BEING "DYED-IN-THE-WOOL?" THIS TERM DERIVED FROM WOOL BEING DYED BEFORE BEING SPUN SO THE THREAD WOULD NOT LOSE ITS COLOR. THE COLOR STAYED "FAITHFUL" TO THE GARMENT.

SHEPHERD'S STAFF

Your parents told you not to talk to strangers, right? The Good Shepherd also tells us not to listen to strangers. We need a Good Shepherd to lead us out and help us examine voices we hear. Are they good or bad? Just as the shepherd goes ahead of the flock, we, too, need to look ahead to where the voices we are listening to will take us. If they are taking us to the unsafe pasture of pride, selfishness, or jealousy—**stop**. Danger is ahead! Ask God to help you. He hears our prayers, goes before us, and will never lead us into a harmful situations. His voice of truth will always lead us to that which is good. When we can't hear the truth, it's wise to wait, be patient, and seek out those who love you enough to tell you the truth. Jesus reminds us in John 14:6— "He is the way, the truth, and the life." His voice will always lead you the right way—the way that leads to life!

Lord, discerning between all the voices in my head can be hard! I pray that You will always gather me into Your arms and lead me into the way, the truth, and the life You have for me. Help me to go ahead and see where my decisions could lead me. If they lead me away from You, it's the wrong direction. I pray to learn how to hear Your voice clearly and to know in my heart that it's You. Lead me, Oh Lord, into the paths of righteousness for Your name's sake. Help me to listen to only Your voice and follow Your lead. Amen.

ART PROJECT:
PERSONALIZED INITIAL FLAGS

ART SUPPLIES

- Fabric
- Pencil
- Scissors
- Elmers Glue
- Twine
- Pom Pom Yarn
- Clothes Pins
- Template of Letters
  (www.thouartexalted.com)

INSTRUCTIONS:

1. Collect different colors of fabric—one for the flag and one for the letter. You want these to be different so they will stand out.

2. Download the flag template (www.thouartexalted.com) and cut out. Using the paper flag as a pattern, trace it onto the back side of your fabric and cut out.

3. Download the alphabet template and find your initials. Using these as a pattern, trace them (with pencil) onto the fabric and cut out.

4. Glue the initial onto the flag using Elmer's glue. Iron to seal the glue when dry.

5. Taking clothes pins, pin the flags onto your twine. (Measure enough twine and cut to the size of your preference.)

6. Hang in your room where you can always be reminded that God knows your name. You are special and unique!

~ All templates can be found on www. thouartexalted.com under the He Knows My Name 20/20 Mini tab.

"These flags remind me that God knows my name. I am an individual, and I don't have to be like anyone else."
- Evelyn (7th grade)

SHEEP DO NOT WORRY

"Look at the birds. They don't plant or harvest or store food in barns, for your heavenly Father feeds them. And aren't you far more valuable to him than they are? Can all your worries add a single moment to your life?"

Matthew 6:26-27 (NLT)

Do you think sheep ever get stressed? I doubt it. What do they have to worry about anyway? They don't have to be anxious about being invited to birthday parties. They don't worry about what they are going to wear to school. They don't get caught up in what other sheep think about them. They don't get tangled in the latest gossip. Their parents don't get divorced or lose their jobs. What is their secret? Sheep continually and completely depend on the protection of their shepherd. He's **in front** of his flock leading them to safe and green pastures. He's **behind** them making sure no sheep get lost. And, he's **with** them taking care of their daily needs. In front. Behind. With. What a difference it makes when we, too, trust in the Good Shepherd.

Abby was not looking forward to going to school. She knew that Jessica was going to ask her to her birthday party, but Abby had already made plans with Isabella. Jessica did not invite Isabella to her party, and Abby didn't want any feelings to be hurt. Abby was worried. She understood why Jessica could not invite everyone to her party, but she made it sound so exclusive. It's not fun being the one left out. Because Abby had experienced this feeling before, she was going to try something she had never done. **Pray.** "Lord, please calm the situation and lead me to say the right things. Thank you for my sweet friendships. I am friends with both Jessica and Isabella, and I want to keep it this way. Worry isn't going to help my stress or help the situation. I need Your help. Lead me and guide me. Guard my heart from wacky emotions and help me to say the right words. Today, I give this situation to you. Amen."

Trusting in the Good Shepherd gives us a peace we cannot explain. In fact, Philippians 4:6-7 says, "Do not worry about anything; instead, pray about everything. Tell God what you need, and thank him for all he has done. Then you will experience God's peace, which exceeds anything we can understand. His peace will guard your hearts and minds as you live in Christ Jesus." Abby knew this to be true. She told God what she needed—help with protecting her friendships. God gave her a peace that in turn gave her confidence to face the day. Worry is never the answer. Prayer is key to living a stress-free life!

1. Why do you think Matthew reminds us that God even takes care of the needs of birds? What lesson does this teach us about trusting God to meet our needs?

----

2. Read Philippians 4:6-7. Why do you think God tells us not to worry? What are the three things that God tells us to do? How will this help us be stress-free?

----

3. Why do you think being thankful is a huge part of getting rid of our worry? What are you worried about today, and how can God's peace guard your heart and mind?

MORE TO CHEW: God gives us Peace ~ Isaiah 26:3, John 16:33, 2 Corinthians 13:11

SHEPHERD'S STAFF

FLOCK FACTS

A SHEPHERD'S STAFF IS USED FOR GUIDANCE. JUST AS THE GOOD SHEPHERD GUIDES US BACK INTO THE FOLD OF HIS PEACE WHEN WE WANDER OFF INTO WORRY, THE SHEPHERD USES HIS STAFF TO NUDGE THE SHEEP BACK IN THE RIGHT DIRECTION.

Worry is something we all do. But worrying about something will never brings us peace. It will only bring us more problems. The word for worry actually means "to choke." Worry chokes out the peace and joy God wants to give us. God wants us to come to Him, pray, and tell Him about our worries. He desires a personal relationship with us and not just an occasional "Thank You for this food" kind of prayer. Being thankful also heals our hearts from worry. How? When we are grateful, our thankful hearts begin to outweigh our worries and our perspective begins to change. Matthew 6:34 reminds us not to worry because tomorrow has enough worry of its own. Let the Good Shepherd lead you today, in this present moment. Stress often comes from worrying about tomorrow. But tomorrow is unknown. The only one who can lead us into tomorrow is Jesus, and only He knows what tomorrow will bring. Instead of worrying, call on the Good Shepherd today.

Lord, You are my Good Shepherd and desire a personal relationship with me. You really do care. You really do want me to talk to You. You really do want me to give You my worries. You don't like to see me stressed because You know the peace You offer when I just trust in Your lead. Why am I so stubborn? Why do I believe worrying will give me more control? That is not the truth. Teach me to give You my worries in exchange for thanksgiving. I pray Your peace will guard my heart and mind. This is the peace I long for—knowing You are in control. Amen.

EARS UP OR DOWN?

"A gentle answer will calm a person's anger. But an unkind answer will cause more anger."

Proverbs 15:1 (ICB)

SHEEP'S CORNER

Do you have a friend who **never** gets angry? Do you have a friend who **always** seems to get angry? What is the difference? I bet it's the way they respond. Anger is a natural defense when we are wronged or feel threatened in some way. Anger is also a response when something seems unfair or undeserved. Have you ever noticed it's easy to get angry when we are tired, hungry, or have had a stressful day? When we get angry, our face gets hot, our heart starts to beat faster, and adrenaline rushes through our bodies. But anger is not necessarily a bad thing, especially when you are angry about something you know is **right.**

Caroline could feel the heat rising to the top of her head. Why did the coach tell the entire team her mom had called him expressing concern that practices were going past 6:30 and interrupting dinner time and homework? Caroline didn't know who to be angry with—her mom for calling the coach or her coach who just embarrassed her in front of all her friends. Caroline was known for her temper and was just about to say something she would have regretted when she remembered what her dad told her about her outbursts. If she responded with kindness and a gentle voice and not reacted with a harsh word, then her anger and perhaps the other person's anger would be softened somehow. It was worth a shot. "Coach," Caroline said, "I bet your mom would have said the same thing. You know moms—they are just looking out for the very best for us!" With that said, her coach apologized for being so rude, and Caroline could feel the anger leave her emotions.

Anger is not bad. It's how we handle anger that gets us in trouble! We all express our anger in different ways, but Proverbs 15:1 gives us some advice we need to tape to our bathroom mirrors. "A gentle answer will calm a person's anger. But an unkind answer will cause more anger" (ICB). Anger only produces more anger. When we lash back with our words, we tend to become more angry. But, if we take a deep breath, count to ten, and speak with a gentle voice, our anger will be diffused. It's like deactivating a live bomb with voice control. The next time you feel like a bomb about to go off, try to respond with a soft answer. It worked for Caroline, and it will work for you!

1. Why do you think a gentle answer will calm a person's anger? Why do you think harsh words stir up more anger?

- -

- -

2. Have you ever been in a situation where you didn't lash out but instead, took a deep breath and responded with a calm voice? How about the opposite?

- -

- -

3. Colossians 3:13 tells us, "Do not be angry with each other, but forgive each other as the Lord forgave you." Why do you think forgiveness is so important?

- -

- -

- -

MORE TO CHEW: God does not Approve Anger~James 1:19-21, Colossians 3:12-17, Ephesians 4:26

FLOCK FACTS

SHEEP SHOW EMOTION MORE THROUGH THEIR EARS THAN THEIR FACE. WHY? SHEEP HAVE MORE MUSCLES IN THEIR EARS! WHEN A SHEEP FEELS ANGRY, HER EARS TEND TO STICK STRAIGHT UP. THIS IS HOW A SHEPHERD KNOWS A SHEEP IS NOT HAPPY!

SHEPHERD'S STAFF

Anger is an emotion we all need to deal with appropriately. Did you know that even Jesus got angry? We see His anger when Jesus cleared the temple of money changers in Mark 11:15-18. Jesus saw the way His Father's temple had been changed from a house of prayer to a place to make money. Jesus was angry for the right reasons. Ephesians 4:26 tells us not to sin in our anger. It's not the anger that is wrong. It's how we deal with it. Proverbs 15:1 tells us a gentle answer will calm a person's anger. To calm can mean to turn away or to lead away. Just like the Good Shepherd who leads us to make the right choices, He can also lead us **away** from making the wrong choices. Why cause hurt when we can bring healing? Why cause pain when we can bring peace? Let's choose to diffuse the bomb of anger by choosing to speak love and forgiveness with kindness—just like our Good Shepherd.

Lord, help me when I get angry. I pray You would give me strength to respond with a kind and soft answer rather than lash out with what's on my mind. I pray to leave unkind answers out of my vocabulary and respond (not react) to my emotional outbursts. I can see why responding with gentleness diffuses the bomb of anger. I pray You will teach me to love and forgive rather than be destructive and hold grudges. Anger can cause such bitterness and resentment. Teach me to love with Your amazing grace. Amen.

THE "ITS" DISEASE

"Get rid of your bitterness, hot tempers, anger, loud quarreling, cursing, and hatred. Be kind to each other, sympathetic, forgiving each other as God has forgiven you through Christ."

Ephesians 4:31-32 (GW)

SHEEP'S CORNER

Have you ever heard of the "ITS" disease? If you googled the name, you might find this description: ITS disease is a common illness and often not diagnosed. The symptoms are bitterness, hot tempers, and anger. If you have ever said the words "I deserve **it**," or "I want **it**," or "I am going to get **it**," chances are you are coming down with the sickness. To get rid of the disease, follow these steps of **generosity**. Step one: Encourage someone. Compliment them on their outfit, tell them what a good friend they are, or write them a note. Step two: Do something kind for someone else. Do a chore that is not yours. Clean the dishes without being asked. Make up your bed or take out the trash. Cut flowers for your mom or friend. Step three: Give away something. Clean up your room and give your extra clothes away to a local charity. Volunteer your time. Save your allowance and donate it to a child in another country. There are many solutions to getting rid of the ITS disease. Being generous with your time, your resources, and your gifts will certainly cure this common illness. But you must be aware, this is not a one-time solution. This pesky disease will relapse in a moment's notice. We must be generous and kind at all times.

Amanda could not stop thinking about what other girls had that she did not. Her list was long. It ranged from brand-name rain boots, luxury vacations to far away places, the latest electronics, to an outdoor hammock. Her mind was fixed on how she could get these things. Amanda's mom was concerned when her attitude started changing. Amanda seemed to have a short temper with her little sister and began to argue over the smallest things. It was time for her mom to step in and make the diagnosis. Amanda had the ITS disease.

Believe it or not, Amanda and sheep have something in common. They both need to be sheared. When a sheep has too much wool, the good shepherd will shear them to cut off the extra wool which frees them from the extra weight. When we are weighed down by the things of this world, our Good Shepherd wants to free us, too. But, it's our choice. Shearing for Amanda means cutting off or getting rid of the things she **wants** but doesn't **need.** We can be freed from the "ITS" disease by choosing to take a good dose of Ephesians 4:32. Be kind to one another, be more sympathetic, and forgive as Christ forgave.

1. Have you ever had the ITS disease, the "I-want-it" sickness? What did you want but didn't need? What kind of medicine did you take to get rid of the sickness?

----

2. "Don't be concerned only about your own interests, but also be concerned about the interests of others" Phil 2:4 (GW). How does this help us get rid of the "ITS?"

----

3. Read Colossians 3:12-13. What does God want us to **put on** when we **take off** anger, bitterness, and quarreling from Ephesians 4:31? How is this helpful?

MORE TO CHEW: God's diagnosis for ITS ~ Philippians 2:3-4, Colossians 3:12-13, Romans 13:14

FLOCK FACTS

SHEEP ARE SHEARED ONCE A YEAR. SOME SHEPHERDS USE SCISSORS WHILE SOME USE ELECTRIC SHEARS. SHEARERS HAVE TO BE CAREFUL NOT TO CUT THE SHEEP. A PROFESSIONAL SHEEP SHEARER CAN REMOVE THE FLEECE IN ONE PIECE!

SHEPHERD'S STAFF

We are all guilty of the ITS disease. And unlike sheep, we need to be sheared more than once a year! The weight of always wanting this and that can become very heavy. It not only weighs us down and changes our attitudes, it also takes our eyes off of the Good Shepherd who lovingly takes care of us. When we pile up selfish behavior, anger, and moodiness, we will topple over just like a sheep with too much wool on its back. And you know what happens when a sheep topples over, right? It cannot get back up! Thank goodness for our Good Shepherd who will be there to flip us back over. We need to get rid of the things that weigh us down and clothe ourselves with "compassion, kindness, humility, gentleness and patience" Colossians 3:12. Romans 13:14 tells us to forget trying to satisfy our selfish desires and clothe ourselves with Jesus. That is the perfect cure for the ITS disease. Take a healthy dose of Jesus today!

Lord, thank You for the cure of the ITS disease. I admit that I fall into the trap of wanting things and becoming consumed with trying to get them. The only problem is that these things will never satisfy. When I find myself always wanting more, my behavior changes and life becomes all about me. Help me to change the channel of wanting things to serving others, being thankful and kind, and forgiving others as You forgave me. Help me to shear off the worldly things that are weighing me down and clothe myself with Your compassion for others. Amen.

FEED YOUR FAITH

"Now faith is being sure of what we hope for and certain of what we do not see. . . . By faith, Moses' parents hid him for three months after he was born, because they saw he was no ordinary child, and they were not afraid of the king's edict."

Hebrews 11:1,23

SHEEP'S CORNER

What would happen if shepherds fed their sheep hot fries, coke, and candy? My guess is they would not make the trek to the next pasture! Why? Junk food slows the body down making us more tired, cranky, and non-responsive. When we eat food that is not healthy for us, we become sluggish. Our bodies were created to eat healthy food that gives us energy. Junk food only zaps the energy right out of us! In order for us **to be** healthy, we have **to eat** healthy. The same is true with our faith. We have to feed our faith with the healthy food of Scripture to prevent our faith from becoming tired, dull, and fearful.

Emily chose NOT to go to youth group. In fact, Emily was embarrassed to tell her new friends at school that she wasn't going to the basketball game because she had to go to church on Wednesday night. What was the point anyway? She could have lots more fun cheering on the Middle School Pirates than learn about Bible verses. Plus, the only food they served at youth group was weird healthy snacks (thanks to a health nut mom). They were all into kale chips, hummus, and red peppers. At least the Middle School offered hot dogs and cotton candy at the game. Why settle for granola when you can have grape soda? Emily just wanted to fit in not stand out.

Faith gets clogged when we are more concerned about what people think about us than what God wants for us. Trying to impress friends is superficial, just like junk food. Emily's fear of not being accepted by her friends dulled her desire to grow in her faith at youth group. **Fear is the junk food of faith**—it stops us from believing God has an amazing plan for our lives. Moses' mother was just the opposite. Her faith and trust in God was not about impressing others. It was about having 100% confidence that God would take care of her family. After the King ordered all boys under the age of two to be murdered, she brushed her fear aside and hid Moses for three months, put him in a basket, and sent him down the Nile river. Moses' mother could not **see** into the future and was not certain of the outcome. But because of her FAITH in God—sure of what she hoped for and certain of what she could not see, she **trusted** in God's plan. Moses was safely found and was raised by Pharaoh's daughter. Emily needs to take a few lessons from Moses' mom!

1. What is the definition of faith according to Hebrews 11:1? How was Emily's faith different from Moses' mother's faith?

_____

2. Why do you think Moses' mothers' faith was so strong? How did her faith cover her fear?

_____

3. Junk food may satisfy short term, but it will eventually give us a tummy ache. What "junk" can be bad for our faith? How can we can become healthier in our faith?

_____

MORE TO CHEW: God's Rx for Healthy Faith~1 Corinthians 16:13, Hebrews 12:12-13, 1 John 4:18

SHEPHERD'S STAFF

FLOCK FACTS

SHEEP ARE GRAZING ANIMALS. THIS MEANS THEY WILL EAT WHATEVER IS IN FRONT OF THEM! GOOD SHEPHERDS WATCH OVER TO MAKE SURE THEY DO NOT EAT UNHEALTHY OR POISONOUS PLANTS.

Hebrews 12:12-13 says, "Lift up the hands which hang down, and the feeble knees; And make straight paths for your feet" (KJV). In order to feed our faith with trust, we need to do three things: Surrender our plans (lift up our hands), get down on our knees and pray (feeble knees), and walk into our situations with faith that God is going to lead the way and take care of us (make straight paths). **Surrender. Pray. Walk.** This is the healthy food that will feed our faith. When we are more concerned with what others think about us, we are not walking in faith but walking in fear. Fear is the granddaddy of spiritual junk food. It slows us down and makes us weak. It makes us doubt God's enormous love for us. We feed our faith by believing and trusting that God is our Good Shepherd.

Surrender. Pray. Walk. Thank You, Lord, that You have taught me how to feed my faith. By giving You my plans and not trying so hard to impress others, You will lead me into the right direction—every time. I pray when I cannot see the path ahead, I will always trust in You. The next time I start to control my day (and popularity), please convict me to put my faith in You. Help me not to eat the junk food of fear but always lead me into healthy pastures! Amen.

ART PROJECT:
PERSONALIZED SHEEP STATIONARY

ART SUPPLIES

- Colorful Stationary Cards and Envelopes • White Paint
- Thin Black Pen (Preferably a Micron Pigma .005 or Thin Sharpie)

INSTRUCTIONS:

1. Buy colorful blank stationary cards with envelopes. The cards used in the photograph are Spr!tz Blank Note Cards. You can find them at Target, Michaels, or online.

2. Buy a thin black Sharpie, or my favorite, a Micron Pigma Pen. Make sure you get the .005 tip.

3. Dip your finger in white paint and add a fingerprint on the card and envelope. There is no right or wrong number of prints. Eventually, these will turn into sheep. You can have one or two, or a whole flock!

4. Let the paint dry! (Very important ~ you don't want to add the black ink until paint is completely dry.

5. While paint is drying, use a piece of paper and draw some sheep. You can use this illustration or be creative.

6. When you have drawn the faces and legs on the sheep, write words that have been meaningful to you in the Bible study. For example: Follow Me. You Know My Name. He is my Good Shepherd. Have fun!

" I love combining art with God's Word because art gives me a visual image of what I am learning and helps me understand what God is teaching me. "

– Maggie Maye
(5th grade)

BLACK SHEEP AND ROTTEN APPLES

"See to it, brothers that none of you has a sinful, unbelieving heart that turns away from the living God. But **encourage** one another daily, as long as it is called Today, so that none of you may be hardened by sin's deceitfulness."

Hebrews 3:12-13

SHEEP'S CORNER

Have you ever heard the phrase, "He/she is the black sheep of the family?" Have you heard, "One bad apple spoils the basket?" These two phrases are similar in meaning. Just as a rotten apple can spread bacteria to the rest of the healthy bunch, a person with a bad attitude can infect everyone around them. Discouragement is contagious. Bad attitudes can spread doubt and fear within a group in seconds. One complaining spirit and the whole plan can be thrown off kilter.

> Melody couldn't believe what she was hearing! Her small group had decided to take their day off school and volunteer at a nursing home. Now one person (name not to be mentioned) was spoiling the whole idea! Angela (oops) starting telling everyone how old people were scary, weird, and ate with their mouths open. Her discouragement spread like wildfire. Now no one wanted to get the service hours they needed to graduate. Melody tried to explain that she had been to this nursing home before and found the men and women to be delightful, funny, and genuine. Her experience was nothing but a huge blessing. But it was too late. Angela's negative influence had sealed the deal. The volunteer opportunity was called off.

God knows all too well that one bad attitude can spoil any plan of action. This is why it is written in Hebrews "See to it . . . ." God wants us to take action and believe that His plan is best. Ask Caleb and Joshua. Just like Melody, they wanted to move forward. They wanted to pursue what God had promised to the Israelites—the land of Canaan. But after a secret mission exploring the land, certain men had different ideas. Read Numbers 13:27-14:9. Caleb and Joshua were excited to take possession of the land God had promised. However, there were some "black sheep" and "bad apples" spreading bad reports. These men discouraged the Israelites by saying, "The people who live there are powerful. The land we explored devours those living in it. All the people we saw there are of great size" (Numbers 13:28, 32). Instead of encouraging the people, they allowed fear to take away their courage. Their unbelieving hearts turned them away from believing in God's promise. Caleb and Joshua were heart broken. They believed God could do anything. But not the bad apples. They spoiled the basket—and the mission into Canaan.

1. Have you ever been in a situation where one person spoiled the plans because of discouragement? Have you ever spoiled plans because you were discouraged?

_____

_____

2. In Numbers 13, how did the people destroy God's plan for them? How did unbelief play a central role?

_____

_____

3. What is sin? How can sin be deceitful and turn us away from God (Heb. 3:12-13)? How does belief and encouragement turn us toward the Living God?

_____

_____

_____

MORE TO CHEW: God's Encouragement ~ 1 Thessalonians 5:11, 14-17, Hebrews 10:23-25

FLOCK FACTS

TRUE OR FALSE?
A BLACK SHEEP ARE USUALLY DISRUPTIVE AND REBELLIOUS.
B. BLACK SHEEP ARE NOT AS VALUED BECAUSE THEIR WOOL CANNOT BE DIED.

ANSWERS: A FALSE B. TRUE

SHEPHERD'S STAFF

Unbelieving hearts turn us away from the Living God and **away from** the amazing plans God has for us. Believing hearts turn us toward the Living God and **toward** the amazing plans God has for us. As believers, we are called to BELIEVE. We are called to **encourage** one another and stand on the promises of God. It is not our job to fear God's plan or to discourage others. We are called to give one another courage! One definition for sin is failing to do what is right. Being led by our fears and not by the promises of God will always steer us down the wrong road. Hebrews 10:23 tells us to "hold unswervingly to the hope we profess, for he who promises is faithful." Yes. **God is always faithful**. If God is in your plans, it will happen. Turn toward the Living God and encourage yourself, your friends, and your family to press through difficulty and discouragement. The Good Shepherd is on your side.

Thank You, Lord, that Your plans are filled with life! When I doubt who You are and where You are leading me, send me someone who will encourage me. Help me also to encourage others when I see them starting to show unbelief. Keep sinful and discouraging thoughts far from my brain. Help me to study Your Word so I will know Your promises. I pray not to be a rotten apple or a black sheep. Help me to be a courageous believer who lives for Jesus and encourages others. Amen.

SHEEP SEEKING WISDOM 101

"If any of you lacks wisdom, he should ask God who gives generously without finding fault, and it will be given to him. But when he asks, he must believe and not doubt, because he who doubts is like a wave of the sea, blown and tossed by the wind."

James 1:5

SHEEP'S CORNER

Shepherds are wise. They know the land and the climate. They know when and where to move the flocks to provide the best food. They know where the streams are to provide water. They know how to prevent injuries and take care of each sheep—individually. They make the best decisions they can. It's their job. Today, **Jesus is our Good Shepherd** who also knows the best decisions for us. He knows the land of middle school, the best food of technology that is healthy for us, and how to prevent us from getting into trouble. He is the definition of wisdom, but it's our choice whether to follow.

Henley had a choice to make between right and wrong. She was spending the night at her friend's house when her friend, Sally, thought it would be a good idea to sneak out at midnight. Henley's heart jumped a beat and she felt sick to her stomach. She didn't want Sally to think she was a chicken, but she knew her parents would be so disappointed in her if she got caught. That was it! IF she got caught. At least, that's what Sally was telling her. Henley got so nervous, her stomach got the best of her and she threw up. She called her Mom to come and get her. When she got home, Henley was thankful her stomach was more wise than her future decision to do something wrong. Better to throw up then make a bad choice.

We all struggle with difficult decisions at some point in our lives. That's why we should always **ask God** to lead us into good decision making. The question becomes: Who do we ask when making a decision between right and wrong? James tells us we should first ask God who promises to give wisdom to us generously. Ask Solomon. He was the wisest man in the Old Testament who sought God's wisdom rather than the advice of men. Read 1 Kings 3:5-15. In Solomon's dream, the Lord came and offered to give him whatever he wanted. Pause. What would you ask for? Just think about it. It's only a dream, right? But even in his sleep, Solomon had wisdom. He asked God for a "discerning heart to govern the people and to distinguish between right and wrong" (1 Kings 3:9). WOW. We can use this prayer as a base for asking God for wisdom, too. Fill in the blanks: God, I pray for a discerning heart to _____ and to distinguish between right and wrong. **Boom**. This prayer has wisdom all over it.

1. Have you ever been in a position like Henley where peer pressure was tempting you to make the wrong decision? What did you do?

----

2. What would you ask for if you had the chance to ask God for anything? Why was wisdom a great choice for Solomon? What else was given to him (1 Kings 3:13)?

----

3. How do you decide between what is right and wrong? Why do you think when we ask God for wisdom we must believe and not doubt or be tossed like a wave?

MORE TO CHEW: God's Wisdom ~ Jeremiah 3:15, James 3:13,17, Ephesians 1:17

SHEPHERD'S STAFF

FLOCK FACTS

SHEPHERDS HAVE TO CHOOSE BETWEEN RIGHT AND WRONG, TOO. THINK ABOUT THE NIGHT THE ANGELS APPEARED TO THEM ABOUT THE BIRTH OF BABY JESUS. IT WOULD HAVE BEEN WRONG FOR ALL THE SHEPHERDS TO LEAVE. SOME HAD TO STAY BEHIND TO WATCH OVER THE FLOCK. GOOD DECISION.

If we look closer at Solomon's prayer, we find three things of importance. First, Solomon remembered God's faithfulness in the **past**. "You have shown kindness to my Father and gave him a son to sit on the throne" (vs. 6). Second, Solomon remembered God's faithfulness in the **present**. "You have made me a King in place of my Father" (vs. 7). Third, Solomon remembered his need for wisdom in his **position**. "I am only a child and do not know how to carry out my duties" (vs. 7). When we are asking for wisdom, we need to remember God's faithfulness in the **past** and **present** so we can have wisdom in our current **position**. In Ephesians 1:17, Paul tells us God is the One who gives us wisdom. "I keep asking that the God of our Lord Jesus Christ, the glorious Father may give you the Spirit of wisdom and revelation, so that you may know him better." Let's use Paul's prayer often so we, too, can KNOW the Good Shepherd better to make good and wise decisions!

Lord, help me to ask YOU for wisdom first before I seek the advice of girl friends (or boys for that matter!) when making a decision. Thank You for the prayer of Solomon that reminds me of Your faithfulness in the past and in the present when I ask for wisdom in my current situation. Thank You also for the prayer of Paul. I want the spirit of wisdom revealing to me who You are. I want to get to know You better. I pray for a discerning heart to learn right from wrong. Thank You, Good Shepherd, for leading me. Amen.

SHEEP KEEP IT FUNNY!

"A cheerful heart is good medicine but a crushed spirit dries up the bones."

Proverbs 17:22

I am not sure if sheep are funny, but one thing is for sure, Presidents can be funny! Did you know that during World War I, President Woodrow Wilson had a flock of sheep on the White House lawn? He wanted to be an example for our nation by contributing to the war efforts. This flock of sheep, numbering 48 at its height, not only kept the White House lawn manicured and fertilized, the wool was auctioned and raised over $52,000 for the Red Cross. That's creative thinking—particularly during a difficult time in America's history. God tells us that keeping a cheerful heart is good medicine for the soul. Some Bible translations substitute the word cheerful for having a happy heart or a joyful heart. Humor seems to soften any circumstance.

> The family trip was going fine until the Smiths picked up the rental car. It was too small for their family of six plus the eight pieces of luggage. Seating arrangements became the highlight of attention and Casey did not want to get in the back . . . again. She was the smallest, but really? Why did she always get tucked between the luggage, snack food, water bottles, and the laundry basket which kept growing by the day? "I'm NOT getting in the back again," Casey cried. "Who cares if I'm the youngest and don't get car sick?" Before the Smiths left the parking lot, there was a heated battle for seat placement. "That's enough," Paula Smith said with her teeth clenched. "You need to be thankful that we are even on vacation. Get in the car. Now!" The Smiths pulled out of the hotel when Paula had a great idea. Just across the street was the Flintstone's theme park. She pulled into the parking lot and made all of her kids get out of the car (with not so happy faces) and pose next to one of the life size figures for selfies. Not realizing what was happening, the kids stood next to Bam Bam, Wilma, and Fred when they all busted out laughing. Laughter is good for the soul and family vacations!

Proverbs tells us that a cheerful heart is good medicine, but a crushed spirit dries up the bones. This was true for the Smith family and for President Wilson. During tense and stressful situations, it's always good to take a deep breath, think creatively, and have a good laugh. It's not always easy. Trust the Good Shepherd and take a dose of what the doctor ordered—laughter!

1. What is medicine, and why do we need it? Why do you think Proverbs tells us a happy heart is good medicine? How?

_____

2. Have you ever been in a position when you needed laughter and creative thinking to break up a stressful moment? Give an example.

_____

3. Proverbs says, " . . . a crushed spirit dries up the bones." Has your heart ever felt crushed or disappointed? How could a cheerful heart have been good medicine?

_____

_____

MORE TO CHEW: God's Medicine ~ Proverbs 15:15, Proverbs 31:25, Ecclesiastes 3:4

FLOCK FACTS

WOODROW WILSON (1913-1921), THE 28TH PRESIDENT OF THE UNITED STATES, BEGAN HIS SHEEP HERDING CAREER BY PURCHASING 18 SHEEP FOR THE WHITE HOUSE LAWN. ONE RAM WAS NAMED OLD IKE AND WAS FAMOUS FOR CHEWING TOBACCO!

SHEPHERD'S STAFF

Even in the toughest of emotional and difficult times, there is always room for a little laughter. Have you ever noticed how you felt after a good belly laugh? A funny movie? A hilarious story? Laughter is proven to boost your heart rate and increase muscle movement while moving more oxygen to your tissue. The negative side of not having laughter in your life is this: It crushes the bones and the spirit. Negative thoughts only increase the already stressful situation and drain you of your strength. Laughter, on the other hand, lessens depression, calms anxiety, and relieves pain. It's the medicine of a cheerful heart that is good medicine for the body! Let's make the choice to be joyful today and trust the Good Shepherd. Even in the difficulties, **God has a plan** and a purpose for our lives. "Be joyful always; pray continually; give thanks in all circumstances, for this is God's will for you in Christ Jesus" (1 Thessalonians 5:16-18).

Lord, thank You for the gift of laughter! Help me today to be creative and have a joyful heart when I face difficult circumstances. Help me to think out of the box and have a cheerful heart. It's hard to be happy when I am emotionally down. Lead me during these times and guide me to joyful people. Thank You Father that I can always trust in Your plan for me, even when all I can see is luggage, stinky clothes, junk food, and back seats. Yes. Laughter is always good medicine. Amen.

STRANGER DANGER!

"Be alert, be on watch! Your enemy, the Devil, roams around like a roaring lion, looking for someone to devour. Be firm in your faith and resist him . . . ."

1 Peter 5:8-9 (GNT)

SHEEP'S CORNER

A sheep's natural instinct is to follow the sheep in front of them. This is both good news and bad news. The good news is when the sheep have a good leader, they will follow in the direction of good. When they follow a bad leader, they can be led into dangerous situations—life or death situations. When sheep leave the flock, they are wide open for wild animals to make their next dinner plans. When sheep are under the care of a good shepherd, they are protected and safe. The same is true with us. When we follow bad leadership, we make poor choices that lead us into risky situations. When we follow good leadership, we make good choices and are protected under the care of the Good Shepherd, Jesus.

Evee was shocked when she saw Nicole at school. Why on earth was she wearing all that make-up? Good gracious. She had so much foundation on that you could not see her God-given freckles. When Evee went up to Nicole to say "Hello," Nicole pretended she didn't see her and started talking to other kids. Nicole had changed. She was hanging out with a different crowd, making poor choices (not to mention that her skirt hem was getting shorter and shorter), and her grades were falling. The worst part about ALL of this was that she was ignoring Evee, her best friend since elementary school. Was trying to be popular worth losing your friendships? Was hanging with the cool crowd worth changing your values? Why was Nicole trying so hard to be accepted at their new school? Evee was frustrated and heart-broken that she was losing her best friend.

1 Peter 5:8-9 tells us to be alert and pay attention to our surroundings. Why? Because the devil is ready to attack. This may seem a bit strange, but it's true. The devil is an enemy of God and does not want you to follow His ways. He will try to lure you away from what's right. Watch out! This is called STRANGER DANGER! There is a reason why sheep stay within the flock. There is safety in numbers where the good shepherd can watch over them, protect them, and keep them safe from roaring lions. Us, too! It's important that we choose the right flock (friends) to be with and stand firm in our faith. While being popular and choosing to go with the cool crowd might look attractive, you could end up being the next meal for a hungry lion.

1. How can seeking friendships for the sole purpose of being popular be like a lion looking for someone to devour?

_____

_____

2. How can we be self-controlled and alert? What are practical ways we can resist the devil and stand firm in our faith?

_____

_____

3. Have you ever followed a bad leader and gotten into a bad situation? How could following a good leader instead have made a difference?

_____

_____

_____

MORE TO CHEW: God's Warning ~ Hebrews 2:1, James 4:7-8, John 10:5, 10-12

SHEPHERD'S STAFF

FLOCK FACTS

DID YOU KNOW THERE ARE CERTAIN SHEEP IN ICELAND WHO ARE KNOWN FOR THEIR LEADERSHIP SKILLS? THESE SHEEP ARE CONSIDERED HIGHLY INTELLIGENT AND HAVE THE ABILITY TO LEAD THE FLOCK DURING DIFFICULT SITUATIONS

I bet your mom told you not to talk to strangers. So does God. If sheep don't listen to the voice of strangers, neither should we. John 10:5 says, "But they will never follow a stranger; in fact, they will run away from him because they do not recognize a stranger's voice." We need to think like sheep. When you hear bad advice, run. When you are tempted to make a bad choice, run. When you are feeling pressured to do something just because it's cool, run. This is **stranger danger!** The enemy, the devil, has one mission in your life—to steal, kill, and destroy your faith in the Good Shepherd. This is why it's very important to guard your faith, stand firm, and stick with the flock. Don't stray away, but find faithful friends who will encourage you and share your beliefs. Jesus came so we may have life and have it abundantly—not be the next meal! Flee to the flock and stay under the protection of the Good Shepherd!

Dear Lord, I don't want to be on the meal plan of the enemy. Help me to know Your voice and to run from anything that is not of You. The enemy is deceptive and wants to lure me away. Help me to discern stranger danger. Give me strength to stand firm in my faith when I am tempted to leave the flock. Provide me with good friends that I can always count on and trust. Friendship are so valuable. Help me to be a good friend, too. Thank you for Your protection over me. I know You love me because You know my name and always lead me into safe pastures. Amen.

ART PROJECT:
GOOD MORNING, GOOD SHEPHERD!

ART SUPPLIES

- 8 x 10 Acrylic Frame (Dollar Tree)
- Scrapbook Paper
- Elmer's Glue
- Elmer's Glue Stick
- Double-Sided Tape
- Scissors
- Pencil
- Hole Punch
- Buttons
- Template (www.thouartexalted.com)
- Fabric cut to 1.5" x 17"
- Optional: Glue Gun

INSTRUCTIONS:

1. Download the template for the Morning Prayer frame (www.thouartexalted.com). Cut out and trace the PURPLE border onto the bottom layer of your scrapbook paper. This is your 8 x 10 base.

2. Repeat step one for the GREEN border, which is the base for your Morning Prayer.

3. After you have cut and traced both layers, cut the blue lines off the Morning Prayer and glue pieces together.

4. Insert the Morning Prayer inside the acrylic frame. Using Elmer's glue (or hot glue), embellish frame with fabric, flowers, and buttons. To make your flower, simply twist your 1.5" by 7" piece of fabric and coil it into a circle (add dots of hot glue to keep it in place). Leave a 5 inch tail to place in your tag.

5. For TAG: Cut out and trace green border onto the base of your scrapbook paper.

6. Cut between the green and grey border of both rectangles on your template and glue the "To" and "From" onto your scrapbook paper.

7. Punch a hole in your tag and weave the tail of your fabric flower through the hole. Secure with glue or double sided tape.

"I read this prayer from the Good Shepherd every morning! It reminds me that He is going to lead my day, and I don't have to worry."
– Winnie (6th grade)

Good Morning Lord!

...is the day that You have made! I will rejoice and be glad in it! As I begin my day, remind me that I am Your masterpiece ...e of a kind. You will never leave my side, and Your love for me will never fail. You have a purpose and a plan for me that is ...ys good. I desire to be a tree PLANTED by streams of water where I can **sit** in Your presence, **stand** on Your promises, and **walk** in Your purposes.

...today with Your Love so that I can live in Joy, Peace, Patience, Kindness, Goodness, Gentleness, Faithfulness, and ...It's easy to get distracted with worry, hardship, and the busyness in my life. Help me to be still and know that ...nd You are God. Help me to pay careful attention to all I have heard in Scripture, especially when I don't think ...have time for You or that You even care. Remove the seeds of doubt so that I do not drift away from the truth ...and into the subtle undertones of unbelief.

...that You have PLANTED Your Word into my heart. Just as a seed cannot grow without the right soil, nutrients, water, and ...I cannot grow in Christ without taking the time to be nourished – absorbing the truths of Your Living Word to sustain ...Lord, let Your Word fall into my heart this morning. I want to be a tree of life that gives wisdom to others. I want to be a ...well-watered tree that invites others to take rest in the shade of my branches.

Lead me today, O Lord, and open my eyes into the wonderful truths of Your Word. I love you I believe in You I put my hope in You. I am PLANTED.

Amen.

TO *Winnie*
FROM: THE GOOD SHEPHERD

PROMISES OF THE GOOD SHEPHERD!

WHEN YOU ARE WORRIED
- Psalm 55:22
- John 14:27
- 1 Peter 5:5-6
- Philippians 4:6
- John 14:1

WHEN YOU NEED HELP
- Psalm 62:8
- Proverbs 3:5-6
- Psalm 33:20
- Psalm 46:1-2
- Micah 7:7

WHEN YOU ARE TEMPTED TO LEAVE THE FLOCK
- 1 Peter 5:8-9
- Hebrews 2:1
- Ephesians 4:1-3

WHEN YOU NEED COMFORT
- 2 Corinthians 1:3-4
- Isaiah 51:12
- 2 Corinthians 7:6

WHEN YOU FEEL ALONE
- Isaiah 41:10
- Jeremiah 30:11
- Matthew 28:20
- 2 Thessalonians 3:3
- Psalm 73:28
- Zephaniah 3:17

WHEN YOU THINK GOD ISN'T ENOUGH
- 2 Corinthians 9:10-11
- Ephesians 1:3-4
- James 1:17-18

WHEN YOU ARE AFRAID
- Psalm 118:6
- Proverbs 3:24
- Nahum 1:7
- Isaiah 43:1

WHEN YOU NEED PATIENCE
- Psalm 27:14
- Psalm 5:3
- 1 Corinthians 13

WHEN YOU DON'T FEEL IMPORTANT
- Ephesians 3:18-19
- Philippians 4:13
- Philippians 1:6
- 1 Peter 4:10

WHEN YOU DON'T FEEL GOD'S LOVE
- 1 John 4:9-10
- Romans 5:5
- Acts 10:4
- Exodus 14:14
- Jeremiah 29:11
- 1 John 4:16
- Romans 8:38-39
- 1 John 4:10-12

PROMISES OF ETERNAL LIFE
- Titus 3:5-6
- Romans 3:22-24
- John 6:47
- Acts 16:30-31
- Romans 10:9-10
- John 11:25-25
- John 3:16-17

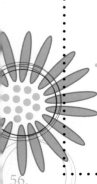

THE GOOD SHEPHERD'S PLAY LIST!

Francesca Battistelli: *He Knows My Name*
Ellie Holcomb: *The Broken Beautiful*
Lincoln Brewster: *Made New*
Casting Crowns: *Who Am I?*
Hawk Nelson: *Drops in the Ocean*
Kari Jobe: *I am Not Alone*
Sidewalk Prophets: *Save My Life*
One Sonic Society: *Never Once*
Matthew West: *You are Everything*
Chris Tomlin: *Our God*
For King and Country: *Fix My Eyes*
Third Day: *Soul on Fire*
Big Daddy Weave: *Overwhelmed*

DOWNLOAD THESE SONGS

FINAL NOTE:

Congratulations—You did it! You finished *He Knows My Name 20/20 Mini Lessons for Girls.* ThouArtExalted would love to continue to pray for you and also know what you learned on this journey. So please keep in touch! There are many ways to find us:

E-Mail: annie@thouartexalted.com
Website: www.thouartexalted.com
Facebook: www.facebook.com/ThouArtExalted
Instagram: anniepajcic
Twitter: @anniepajcic

We are always posting fun ways to learn about Jesus in a creative way. We love you and are praying that the Good Shepherd will continue to lead you, guide you, and show you His way.

Love,
~The ThouArtExalted Team

"HE CALLS HIS OWN SHEEP BY NAME AND LEADS THEM OUT." JOHN 10:3

ArtBox in Your InBox was developed with pre-teen and teenage girls in mind. ArtBox is a CREATIVE devotional lesson that comes directly to your inbox EACH MONTH. This new **digital** resource offers girls the chance to study God's Word and deepen their relationship with Jesus. ArtBox is also filled with fun art projects, memory verses, recipes community service ideas, and more!

Each issue of ArtBox in Your InBox offers:

- 12 monthly PDF devotional lessons with real-life application
- A FUN and CREATIVE art project to reinforce Scripture
- Scripture memory verses
- Additional creative activities such as recipes, community service projects, conversation starters, Christian music playlists, and more

ThouArtExalted is introducing a FREE app for tween and teen girls to read through the New Testament in ONE YEAR! Each day, girls will receive a quick devotional right to their phones that will highlight verses from each chapter of the New Testament starting with Matthew. Packed with fun downloadable graphics, journal questions, prayers, personal application, and YES, art projects along the way—this app will be available January 1st, 2017!

James: Following God's Road Signs is a 27-week Bible Study on the book of James for Middle School girls and boys. It is written to encourage and deepen faith when life isn't quite so easy. God is on our side and gives us INSTRUCTIONS for how to navigate—even when we choose to drive our own way often finding ourselves on a dead end street. The book of James is a **road map** guiding us in the right direction. *Following God's Road Signs* teaches us to put our FAITH INTO ACTION by stopping, looking at God's map, and asking Him for directions. This study is great for youth groups, small groups, and homeschool groups.

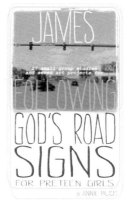

What You Get:
- Study The Book Of James Verse-By-Verse In A Fun, Creative & Preteen-Friendly Way
- 27 Exciting Bible Lessons
- **Creative Art Projects**
- Dig-Deep Discussion Questions
- Lessons Come In a **Digital PDF** Format For Easy Sharing

ThouArtExalted's **FIVE** Small Group Series are easy *five-week* studies for Tween and Teen girls featuring *five lessons* and one art project for *five dollars* (each student booklet). Studies include:

- Seed To Sow
- Love is ALL you Need
- The In and Out Cafe: Jealousy is NOT on the Menu
- Project 2911
- Brave: The Battle Against Tough Stains is Over
- The Perfect Present

Annie Pajcic lives in Jacksonville, Florida with her husband and four children. Using her background in youth ministry, art, and graphic design, she started ThouArtExalted in 2007. ThouArtExalted is a non-profit 501(c)(3) ministry inspiring women and girls to live creatively for Christ. When Annie doesn't have paint on her hands, she is writing and designing Bible studies, picking up kids, cooking dinner, or feeding the chickens. Visit her website at **www.thouartexalted.com** for speaking engagements, art ideas, Bible studies, service projects, and devotionals.

72592288R00035

Made in the USA
Columbia, SC
21 June 2017